Leaf Man

Lois Ehlert

Harcourt, Inc.

Orlando   Austin   New York   San Diego   Toronto   London

Printed in Singapore

Leaf Man used to live near me,

in a pile of leaves.

But yesterday the wind blew Leaf Man away.

He left no travel plans.

The last time I saw him,

he was headed east— past the chickens,

toward the marsh, over the ducks and geese.

A Leaf Man's got to go where the wind blows.

He blew over the fields

of pumpkins and winter squash,

and flew over   the turkey,

past potatoes, carrots, and cabbages in rows.

Then he blew out of sight.

Is he drifting west, above the orchards?

Or over the prairie meadows,

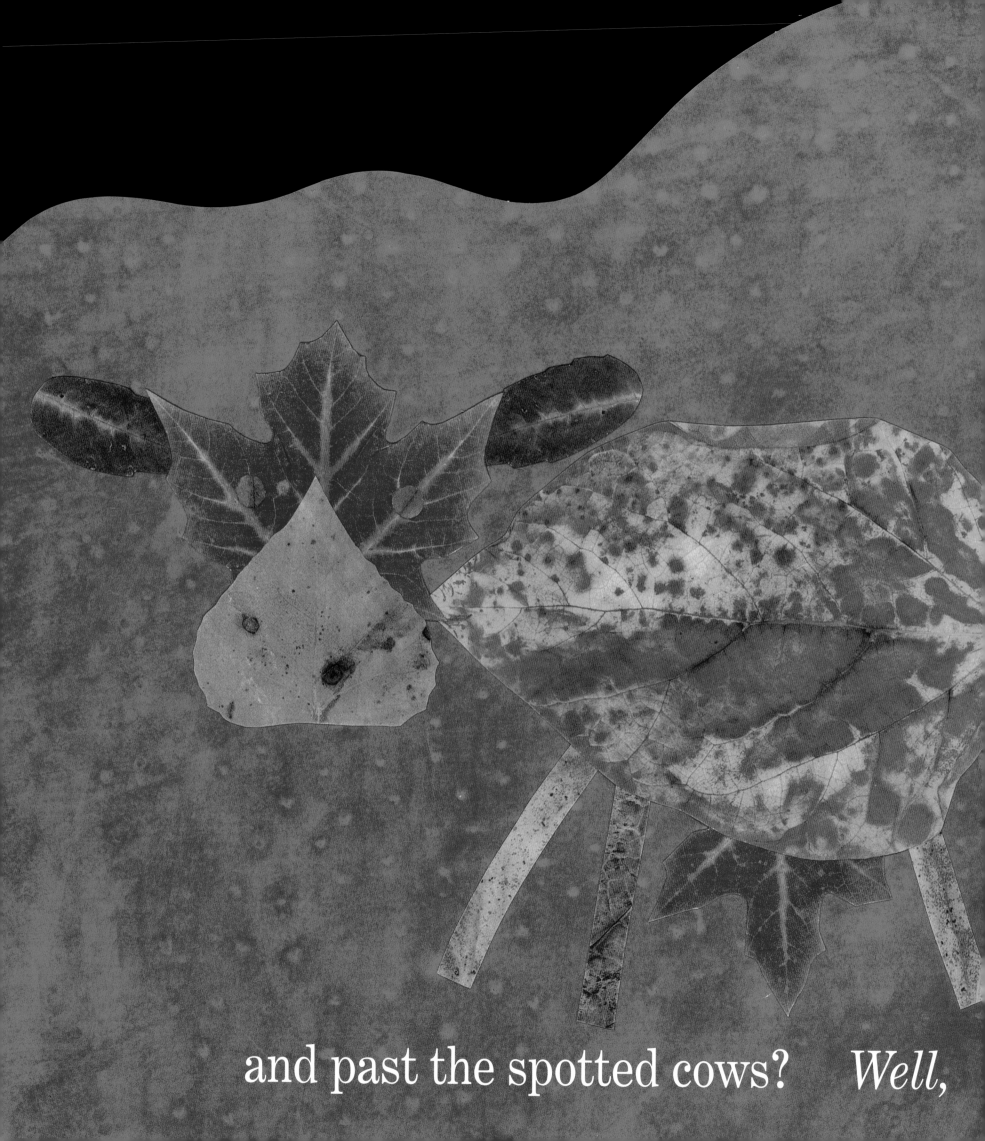

and past the spotted cows? *Well,*

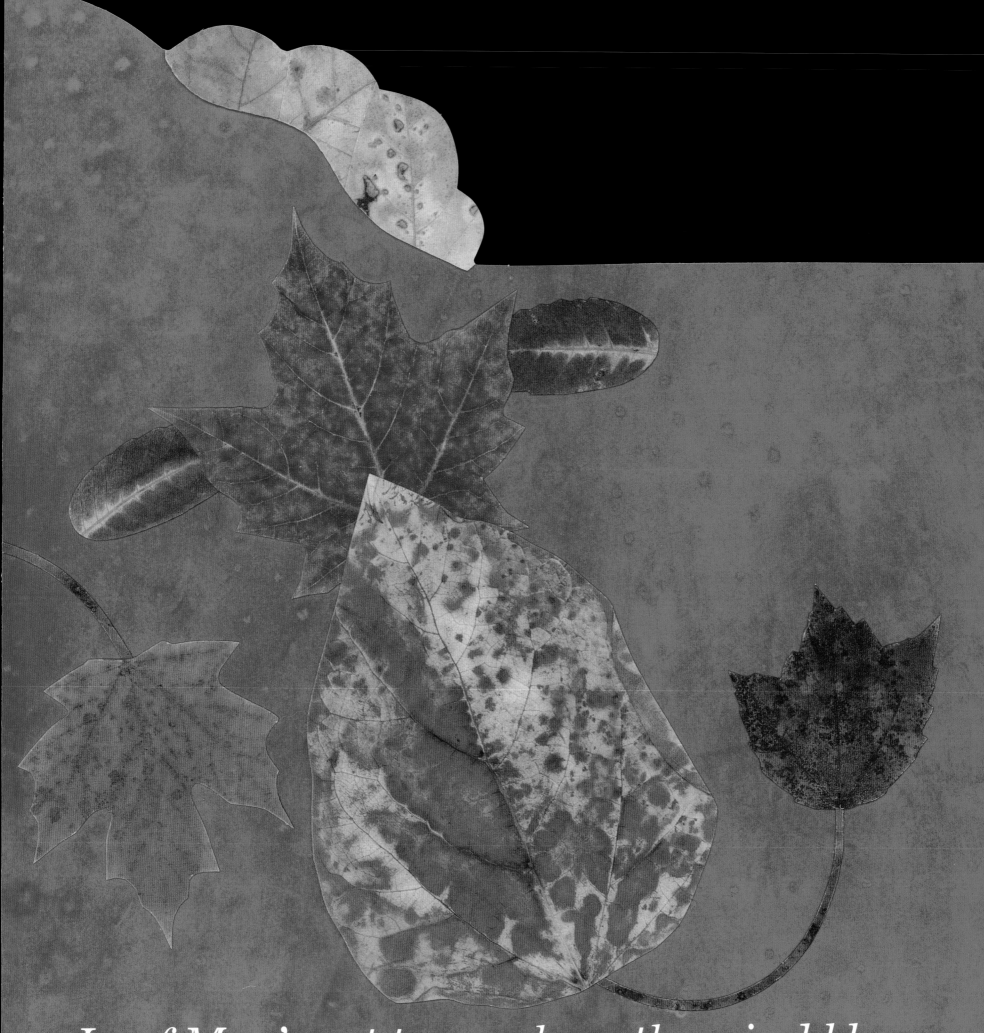

a Leaf Man's got to go where the wind blows.

Maybe Leaf Man's gliding

on a lake breeze,

or flying along the river,

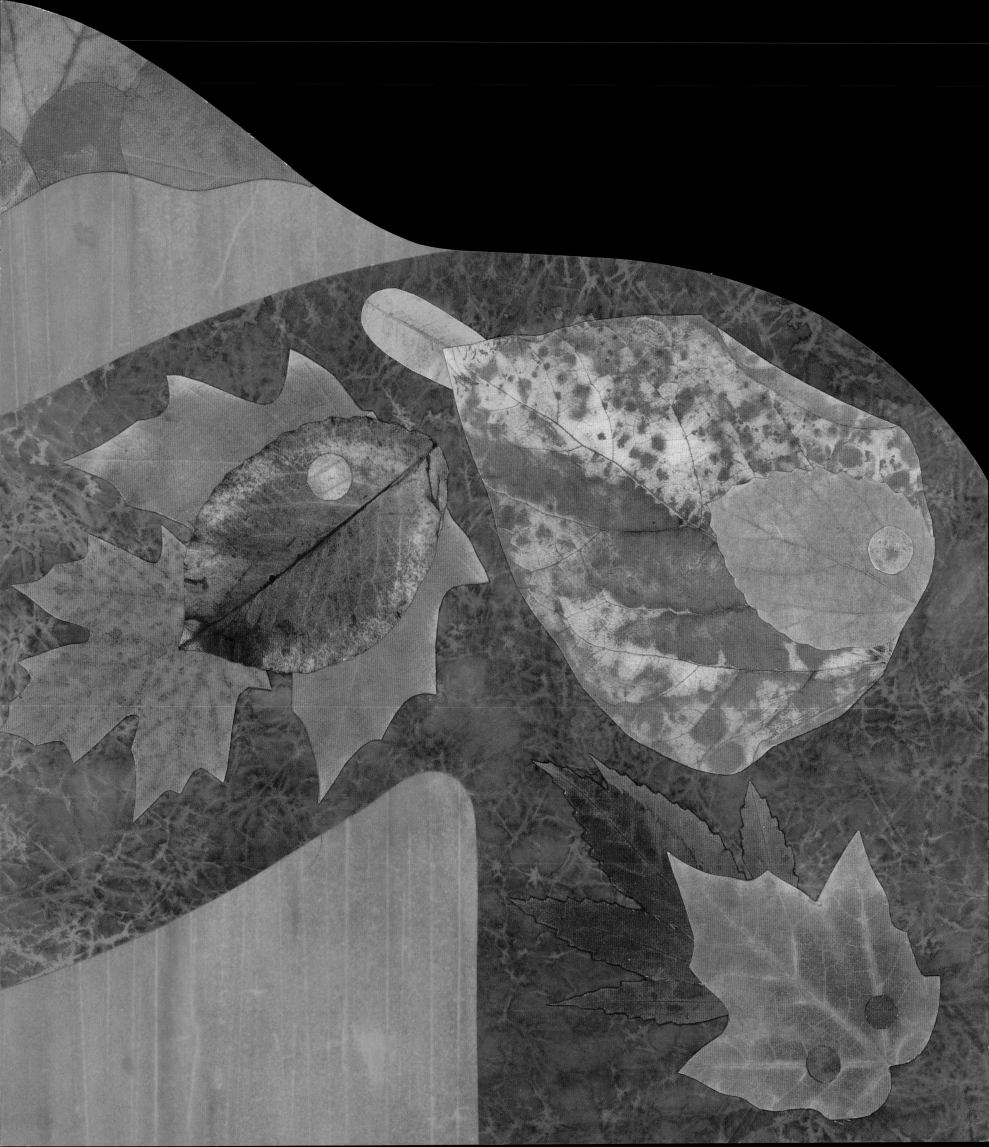

following butterflies going south.   *Well,*

a Leaf Man's got to go where the wind blows.

He might even be traveling north,

above leaves that look   like him,

or flying over mountains,

with a flock of birds.

When Leaf Man looks down on earth,

is he lonesome for a home?

This I *do* know:
Where a Leaf Man
will land, only the wind knows.

So listen for a rustle in the leaves.

Maybe *you'll* find a Leaf Man waiting to go home with you.